Don't Forget!

Halloween

Monica Hughes

Heinemann
LIBRARY

www.heinemann.co.uk/library
Visit our website to find out more information about **Heinemann Library** books.

To order:
 Phone 44 (0) 1865 888066
 Send a fax to 44 (0) 1865 314091
 Visit the Heinemann Bookshop at www.heinemann.co.uk/library to browse our catalogue and order online.

First published in Great Britain by Heinemann Library, Halley Court, Jordan Hill, Oxford OX2 8EJ, a division of Reed Educational and Professional Publishing Ltd. Heinemann is a registered trademark of Reed Educational and Professional Publishing Ltd.

OXFORD MELBOURNE AUCKLAND JOHANNESBURG BLANTYRE GABORONE IBADAN PORTSMOUTH NH (USA) CHICAGO

Designed by Joanna Sapwell and StoryBooks
Illustrated by Tony Randall
Originated by Ambassador Litho Ltd
Printed by Wing King Tong, Hong Kong, China

ISBN 0 431 154031
06 05 04 03 02
10 9 8 7 6 5 4 3 2 1

British Library Cataloguing in Publication Data
Hughes, Monica
    Halloween. – (Don't Forget)
    1. Halloween – Juvenile literature
    I.Title
    394 . 2'646

Acknowledgements
The Publishers would like to thank the following for permission to reproduce photographs: Bridgeman Art Library/British Library p. 7; Bridgeman Art Library/Harris Museum & Art Gallery p. 8; Collections/Brian Shuel pp. 18, 10, 13; Corbis pp. 5, 12, 14, 15, 25, 29; Corbis Sygma p. 23; Corbis/Cynthis Hart p. 24; Corbis/Kevin Fleming p. 28; Getty Images p. 22; Getty Images/Foodpix p. 27; Getty Images/Stone p. 20; Jenny Bentley p. 19; Photodisc pp. 4, 9; Trevor Clifford pp. 16, 17, 21, 26.

Cover photograph reproduced with permission of Bubbles Photo Library.

Our thanks to Stuart Copeman for his assistance in the preparation of this book.

Every effort has been made to contact copyright holders of any material reproduced in this book. Any omissions will be rectified in subsequent printings if notice is given to the Publishers.

Contents

Words printed in bold letters, **like this**, are explained in the Glossary.

What is Halloween?

Halloween is celebrated on 31 October. At this time of year there can be early morning mists and the air is beginning to feel the chill of winter. For thousands of years it was a time when people were afraid that the summer sun had gone forever and that the cold, gloomy winter had come to stay. They were very **superstitious** and afraid of **spirits**, **witches** and **ghosts**, especially at Halloween.

Halloween is now a time of fun and games, especially for children. There is a lot of opportunity to dress up in scary costumes, eat spooky food, play traditional games and actually enjoy being frightened!

Halloween happens in the autumn

Children ready for a Halloween party

For more than a thousand years 1 November has been a special day called All Saints' Day or All-Hallows. The day after All-Hallows was named All **Souls**' Day and this was set aside to remember family and friends who had died.

The night before All-Hallows is 31 October, and was known as All-Hallows **Eve**. The name gradually changed to All-Hallows Even (evening) or Hallowe'en, and finally to Halloween.

Mexican Halloween

In Mexico a festival called *Los Dias de los Muertos*, Days of the Dead, takes place on 1 and 2 November. It is a time for remembering and celebrating the lives of people who have died.

When was the first Halloween?

Celebrations have been held around the time of Halloween for thousands of years. The ancient **Celts** saw the beginning of November as the start of their New Year and the beginning of winter. They celebrated the end of the old year at about the time of year we now celebrate Halloween. They celebrated with a **spirit** festival or festival of the dead, which they called 'Samhain'. The Celts thought that Samhain was a special time when the spirits of the dead could come back to visit their living relatives.

Samhain was thought to be a frightening night when spirits, **ghosts**, demons and horrible beasts wandered around and caused trouble. People lit fires to keep the good spirits warm and to frighten away any evil spirits that came near. They also wore ghostly masks so that any spirits they met would be frightened away.

An artist's idea of a Celtic settlement

The Knight and the Spectre painting by Richard Doyle (1824–83)

At Samhain families remembered their **ancestors**. They believed the Lord of the Dead judged all the dead **souls** during the festival. They offered gifts to him to help him to judge their spirits kindly.

What is Samhain?

Samhain (pronounced sow-en) was also known as Summer's End. It was the end of the Celtic year that began with May Day, or **Beltane**. It was usually celebrated on the night of a **full moon** and after the first proper frost.

What is Pomona Day?

The Romans held a festival known as Pomona Day at the same time of year as the **Celts** celebrated Samhain. After the Romans came to Britain around CE 43 the two festivals began to merge. The Roman festival was dedicated to Pomona, the Roman **goddess** of fruit trees. The apple was also a **symbol** of love for the Romans and a symbol of **immortality** for the Celts. Because of this apples became an important part of the celebrations at the end of October.

A tapestry of Pomona made in about 1885

Allan apples

Halloween is also known as Allan Day. In Cornwall, Allan apples are thought to bring good luck to anyone who eats them. All the local children are given a present of an Allan apple on Allan Day.

Apples were thought to be **holy** or magical. If an apple is cut crossways, a perfect five-pointed star is visible in the place where the seeds are found. The star is the ancient symbol of magic and protection. A star is also a symbol of hope for the future.

Some people thought that the gods stayed young and beautiful by eating apples. The Celts also believed that there was a perfect apple land called **Avalon** where the gods lived.

Apples are sometimes thought to be lucky

Why do we light bonfires at Halloween?

The lighting of huge fires has been an important part of Halloween celebrations since earliest times in Britain. The fires were lit to frighten away bad **spirits** and keep good spirits warm. They were also lit to **honour** the Sun. People thought that the coming of winter and the long dark nights meant that the Sun was losing its power. Bonfires were lit to give the Sun strength to survive through the winter.

A torchlit procession at Halloween

In some places torches were lit from the Halloween bonfire and carried in torchlight processions. Farmers sometimes carried flaming torches to every corner of their fields as a way of scaring away any evil spirits.

Bonfires at Halloween were a very good way of getting rid of all the rubbish such as dead plants and fallen leaves that cover the ground in October. The ash from the Halloween bonfires used to be scattered on the fields. Ash is a good fertilizer, which means it is good for the soil. So the Halloween bonfires helped the next season's crops grow.

Celtic bonfires

Fire was very important to the **Celts**. They used it to cook on and also to keep warm. Often at Samhain the Celts would put out their house fires. They would then relight their fires from a flaming branch taken from the Samhain bonfire. This was to celebrate the start of a new year and to make sure the goodness and strength of the Sun came back the next year.

Who started making Halloween lanterns?

The **custom** of making lanterns out of pumpkins probably started in Ireland. Those lanterns were made out of turnips. The turnips were hollowed out and jagged teeth and wild staring eyes were cut out of them. The lanterns, with candles placed inside, were then put on gateposts and in trees. Sometimes the lanterns were carried round the village by small groups of people wearing masks.

The lanterns were thought to keep away demons and evil **spirits** that were afraid of the light. They were also thought to scare away any **witches** that might be out at Halloween.

In some places they are called Jack O' Lanterns and can have either frightening or friendly faces. The story of Jack O'Lantern is told on page 20.

Pumpkin lanterns

Punky night at Hinton St. George, Yeovil, Somerset

Pumpkins originally came from the USA but they are now very common in British shops and supermarkets at Halloween.

Punky Night

In Hinton St. George, near Yeovil, Somerset, lanterns called 'punkies' are made out of mangel worzel vegetables. A face, an animal or a flower pattern may be cut into them. Children collect money for charity carrying their punky lanterns. The boy and girl who collects the most money is then crowned Punky King and Queen. Punky Night is celebrated on the last Thursday in October.

Trick or treat!

The idea of playing tricks at Halloween is very old. At one time the tricks were blamed on the evil **spirits** thought to be around at Halloween. Tricks included whitewashing windows, blowing smoke through keyholes or smearing treacle on doorknobs. In some places people called 'guisers' (from the word **disguise**) went from house to house asking for food or money at Halloween. They dressed up in frightening masks and disguises, and people treated them well to avoid them coming back.

Children ready to play trick or treat

Scary faces
on Halloween

Today, children often play tricks on people at Halloween. They wear frightening costumes and play a game called trick or treat. They knock on the door of a friend. When the door is opened the children ask to be given a 'treat' of sweets, biscuits, crisps or fruit. If they don't receive a treat then they will play a 'trick' on the person. The tricks are quite harmless and fun for everyone.

Rules for trick or treat:

- Always go in a group with a responsible adult in charge.
- Only call on friends and people you know.
- Always wear a suitable Halloween costume.
- Remember to say 'thank you'.
- Do not play tricks that are dangerous or could cause damage.

Fortune telling at Halloween

Many games played at Halloween were thought to **predict** what might happen in the future. Because the **Celts** thought Halloween was the last night of the year they believed it could show them glimpses of the future.

Apples were used for telling **fortunes** at Halloween. An apple had to be peeled in one long unbroken piece. The peel was then thrown over the left shoulder. It was thought that the peel would land in the shape of a letter. This was supposed to be the first letter of the name of the person they would marry.

Apple-peel letter on Halloween

Trinkets were often hidden in cakes on Halloween

In some places small **trinkets** were baked inside cakes at Halloween. If a girl got a trinket in her piece of cake then she had a clue to the future. A ring meant she would marry soon, a coin meant she would be rich, but a thimble meant she would never marry.

Fortune nuts!

In some places Halloween is known as 'Nut Crack Night'. Hazelnuts were thought to have magical powers and were used as a way of telling people's fortunes at Halloween. Couples placed two nuts side by side in the Halloween bonfire. If the nuts burnt happily together in the fire then they would have a happy marriage. If the nuts jumped out of the fire, the couple would part.

17

What games can you play at Halloween?

Children can play many games at Halloween. Lots of games are played with apples. Apple bobbing is played with apples floating in a large tub of water. The players have to keep their hands behind their back as they kneel down in front of the water. Then they have to try and pick up an apple using only their teeth.

Snap Apple is played by hanging apples on long pieces of string from a doorway. The players have to try and eat a whole apple without touching it, except with their teeth. It can be made even harder by putting some jam or honey on the apple. This will add to the fun!

Apple bobbing

Vampire Chase is a more modern Halloween 'tag' game. One player is a vampire (with a suitable mask and cloak). The other players wear three red sticky labels each. The vampire chases after his **victims** and when he catches one he pretends to 'suck their blood' (takes a red sticker). When a victim has lost all three stickers they then become the vampire and the game carries on.

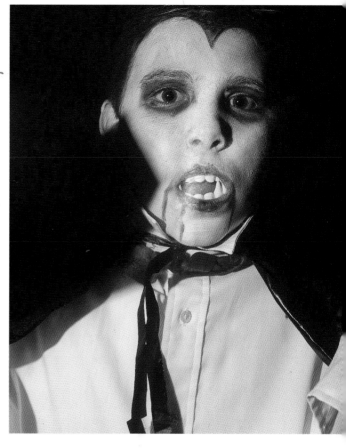

A frightening vampire costume

Have you ever played Musical Bats?

A plastic bat is passed round a circle of children while music is played. When the music stops the person who is holding the bat leaves the ring. The last one left in the circle is the winner and keeps the toy bat as a prize.

19

Halloween stories

A very old story tells of Jack who was so naughty that when he died his **spirit** was not wanted in heaven or hell. Jack's spirit was said to be wandering around and could be seen as a ghostly light flickering at night over marshland. His spirit was said to be out to trick any travellers who were about . The travellers might follow the glow of Jack's lantern thinking they were walking towards safety. Instead they would be led to their death in the marshes. Jack gave his name to the turnip lanterns made at Halloween that are called Jack O'Lanterns.

A ghostly Halloween night

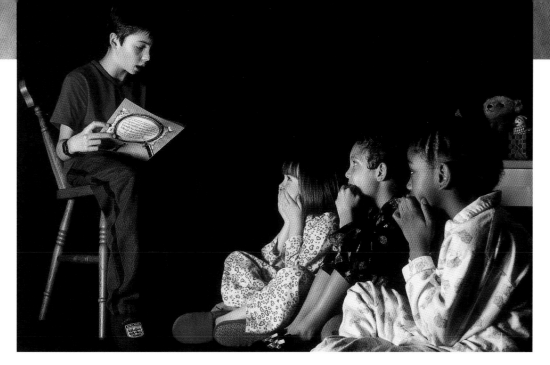

Children listening to a ghost story

Today there are many popular children's stories about **ghosts**, **witches** and skeletons. Most of them are very enjoyable but can sometimes seem rather frightening if read in the spooky atmosphere of Halloween night. Perhaps Halloween is a time to enjoy being frightened!

Vampire stories

In 1897 Bram Stoker wrote a frightening story about a **vampire** called *Count Dracula*. The story was based on Prince Vlad, the ruler of a country called Transylvania. He was a frightening person who was known as Vlad Dracula. The word '*dracul*' means a dragon or a devil.

Who can you dress up as at Halloween?

Years ago people were afraid of the **witches** and evil **spirits** that were thought to roam around at Halloween. Nowadays most people do not believe in witches and evil spirits, but they enjoy dressing up as them, especially when playing trick or treat or going to a fancy dress party.

Lots of children dress up as witches at Halloween and wear a long black robe and tall black pointed hat. A false nose and false fingernails can be added. Some also carry a broomstick or a book of magic spells.

All dressed up and ready for a Halloween party

Ghostly children

Ghost costumes, made out of an old white sheet are also popular, especially if the ghost makes scary wailing noises! Pretending to be a **vampire** is also popular. A vampire was supposed to be a **corpse** that came alive and sucked the blood of someone while they were sleeping. Many children dress up as Count Dracula and wear false vampire teeth, with fake blood dripping from them.

It can also be fun to dress up as a skeleton or a mummy. A mummy is a dead body that has been **embalmed** and covered in bandages. A devil costume will usually be red and include a long cloak and a pair of horns.

What are werewolves?

Some people dress up as werewolves at Halloween. The word 'werewolf' means man-wolf. A werewolf is found in some scary stories, and is a person who changes into a wolf when there is a **full moon**.

Halloween animals

"Friendly Fairy, Witch, or Fay Fulfil the Wish You wish to day."

HALLOWE'EN

A Halloween postcard from 1912

Many different animals have been associated with Halloween. Black cats were thought of as **witches**' cats and regarded as lucky. Even today a black cat crossing your path is thought to be especially lucky. But in some places a white cat is lucky and a black cat is unlucky!

Spiders were thought to be lucky or unlucky depending on when they were seen. An evening spider was lucky but a morning spider was not! It was thought to be very unlucky to kill a spider at any time. Spider's webs are often seen as rather spooky. They are easy to see outside on misty autumn mornings, and inside in dark corners and empty rooms.

Spooky bats

Long ago, bats were seen to swoop around the Halloween bonfire and it was thought they were seeking out the **souls** of the dead. They were probably just trying to catch flies and insects!

People believed owls swooped down to take away the **spirits** of the dying. Because of this, if owls were heard hooting during the night at Halloween, it was considered to be unlucky. It was even worse if they were heard during the day. People became very scared. However, finding an owl's feather is thought to be very lucky.

People used to think owls were frightening

25

What can you eat at Halloween?

Special food can be made at Halloween to remind people of the many traditions linked to the celebrations. The food can be funny because it looks revolting but can still taste delicious!

How about making eyeball jelly! It is made with blackcurrant jelly mixed with a little water. Get an adult to open a tin of **lychees** for you. Then stir them into the jelly. The 'eyeballs' look very spooky but taste super.

Skeleton biscuits are easy to make. Get an adult to help you bake some gingerbread men. Then decorate them by **piping** white icing on them in a skeleton pattern. Icing can also be used to make a spooky spider's web on a

Special food to enjoy at Halloween

plain biscuit or cake. A plastic spider could be added to make the web look even more frightening!

Witch's brew is a drink made by mixing fizzy lemonade with black grape juice. Grapes and pieces of apple are added and these then look like eyeballs and teeth. A straw with a black paper tassel can be used to stir the brew and will look like a magic broomstick.

A pumpkin ready to be made into a Halloween lantern

Pumpkin snacks

The seeds of a pumpkin can be eaten, making a Halloween lantern a tasty snack. Wash the seeds, then lay them on a greased baking tray and get an adult to put them in a hot oven for about 10 minutes or until golden brown. Pumpkin flesh can also be used to make pumpkin pie and pumpkin soup.

27

Halloween around the world

In the USA and Canada Halloween is a very popular time with both children and adults. Trick or treat is a common game and special bags are made to collect all the treats. Everywhere people dress up. Some of them may wear spooky costumes or they may be dressed as popular cartoon characters. Shop windows are decorated for Halloween and there are lots of special things to buy. Families sometimes have special Halloween parties and perhaps pretend that part of their house is **haunted**.

A house decorated for Halloween in the USA

In parts of Europe and South America Halloween is still very closely linked to All Saints' Day and All **Souls**' Day on 1 and 2 November. People remember friends and family who have died by lighting candles and saying prayers. They send cards and visit relatives' graves to place flowers on them. They may also eat special 'soul cakes' made in the shape of a skull or grave.

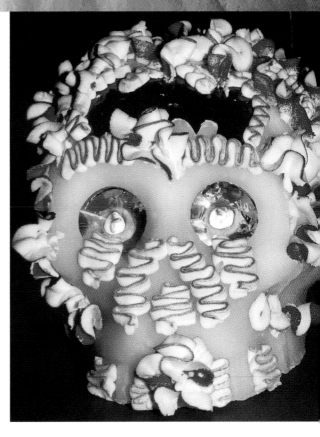

A soul cake from Mexico

Halloween words

Lots of words used at Halloween come from languages other than English:

ghoul   means evil **spirit**, and comes from an Arabic word

zombie   means a **corpse** that has come alive, and comes from a West African language called Bantu

phantom   means a **ghost**, and comes from French.

29

Glossary

ancestors   relations who lived a long time ago

Avalon   land in Celtic legend thought to be paradise

Beltane   Celtic name for a celebration held on 1 May

CE   Common Era, often written as AD

Celts   people who lived in ancient Britain before the Romans came

corpse   dead body

custom   usual way of doing things

disguise   way of making a person look different so they are not recognised

embalmed   way of preserving a corpse so it doesn't decay

eve   day before an important day

fortune   luck a person may have in the future

full moon   when the moon is visible as a complete circle, about once a month

ghosts   spirits of the dead who are thought to haunt people

goddess   female god

haunted   place visited by ghosts

holy   to do with God

honour   give praise and respect

immortality   living forever

lychees   sweet round fruit that has white flesh when peeled

piping narrow lines used to decorate something

predict say what will happen in the future

soul part of a person believed to go on living after death

spirits souls of people who have died

superstitious belief in something not based on evidence

symbol sign with special meaning

trinkets small ornaments or pieces of jewellry

vampire ghost or corpse believed to suck blood from living people

witch woman thought to have magic powers

Index